ESCAPING THE DARKNESS OF MY HEART

Kendra J. Williams

authorHOUSE®

AuthorHouse™
1663 Liberty Drive
Bloomington, IN 47403
www.authorhouse.com
Phone: 1-800-839-8640

Published by AuthorHouse 10/29/2014

ISBN: 978-1-4969-4570-9 (sc)
ISBN: 978-1-4969-4569-3 (e)

DEDICATION

To my mother who has always pushed me to become exactly what I dreamed of. She has always told me the word can't does not belong in your vocabulary.

"In the mist of any storm you are not alone." ~Kendra

CONTENTS

Alone You Are Not 2
Angry 3
The Mountain 4
Day and Night 6
END 9
Forgiveness 11
Healing 13
I Don't Care 15
I thought 17
Leaving This 21
Left 23
Let These Words 25
No More 28
Observe 31
One 33
See through 36
Silence 37
Stress 38
Take This 40
The Fight 46
Sky 50
The Way it Happened 52
There may be a twice 54
Tired 56
To Wait 57
Stop 60
What good is love… 61
What will the next hour bring? 63
Why Can't I Let Go 65
I AM Worthy 68
You can't keep trying to tell yourself you love this person… 73
You told me 77
About the Author 79

Tears don't always mean sadness
And tears don't always mean fear
Tears are a form of letting go
Letting go
Doesn't happen overnight
Healing doesn't take place in one day
The reflection in the mirror tells a story of strength
You have yet to discover this strength
But it's there
Within
Deep down inside
With each day
Grows a newfound love for life
This is just the beginning of the storms to come
It's up to you if you want to weather it or not
The reflection in the mirror
Shows the weakest thought
"You're only as strong as your weakest thought"
Look around
Next to you sits
Someone that has been hurting too
You are not alone
Alone you are not
Wipe the tears away with laughter
Your heart is heavy
And heavy is your heart
But alone you are not

ALONE YOU ARE NOT

ANGRY

Yes that Facebook status is about you
You ugly
But she is uglier
It's not the appearance
But the way she carries herself
The cockiness
The no doubt
The strong statements
The way she speaks
That mirror you are looking in
Isn't full length
You don't need the full length for the appearance of the outer beauty
But the inner beauty as well
You think its about outer
When its about the inner
Those scars you have
On your legs are from inner anger
You are angry about the status
Not because its mean
But because its true
You can't let them see your anger
Because it will register
And hit home
You can't keep throwing yourself into doors and walls
You are going to physically beat yourself down
The mentally has already reached home
Take that anger
And talk to somebody
Everybody isn't writing about you
You can't get mad if the truth hurts
The truth hurts sometimes
Angry
Once you seek help will not be you any longer
Pass that on to someone else

THE MOUNTAIN

Climbing the mountain
It's like climbing a mountain
Steep, unsteady and unstable
Things start falling
And the nerves start overreacting
Shaking
Your legs buckle
You realize it's like no other
It's a constant reminder
By just thinking about the many ones before
You stumble
Almost falling
But you hold your own
Then you notice your heart fluttering
Skipping beats
Then returning to normal
You decide to take a load off
To try to reminisce
But that's no help
Putting all your burdens on someone else's shoulders
Is what seems right
They won't listen
But maybe he/she will
The mountain seems steeper
But you'll overcome
Beating all the odds
Facing the top is all you can envision
But maybe reaching the top
Isn't for your benefit
But for someone else's
Taking note
You try taking another load off
But now it's all up to you
Seeing that now you can make all things right

You grab the top
And at the top lies
The bottom of all bottoms
Your heart sinks
And your mind cries out
Escaping the inside
The tears reach outside
Your eyes overflow
And in an instance
All things add up
The mountain top
Released all your stress and past
And now it leads a way to a future
A future for you to fill
There lay many more mountains to climb
And explore in the near distance
The steep, unsteady and unstable
The mountain

DAY AND NIGHT

She who does speak
Will not be seen
That one
Yes that one
The one with all the words
Yes her
She doesn't have actions
Just words
They aren't noticing her
But that other one
All eyes are on her
She hasn't muffled a word
Yet they are noticing how she moves
She has cried
Behind the smiles and they noticed
She has hidden
Behind the makeup
They noticed
She has lost 5 pounds
Clothes are falling off
They notice
But the other one
She hasn't acknowledged anyone
She has just continued to talk
To continue to use her words
They hear her but aren't looking her
Because she wants attention
She who seeks attention
Will get overlooked
She has officially stopped talking
And yes she is now alone
She didn't notice before
Because she was too self-absorbed
She used her words

To end up alone
Don't talk yourself
Into trouble but act and move
Your way out
She didn't know
Until she finally stood alone
One day the talker
Will become the actor
But until then
She will stand alone
The difference between night and day

Don't
Don't live for them
Live for you
Don't love for them
Love for you
Don't cry for them
Cry for you
Don't give for them
Give for you
Don't understand for them
Understand for you
Don't listen for them
Listen for you
Don't be you for them
Be you for you
Don't write for them
Write for you
Don't speak for them
Speak for you
Don't do this for them
Do this for you

Remember whatever you do in life, make sure it's completed for you and your conscience no matter how hard it is for you to do.

END

Many things come and go
Just like a phase in life
Some things we all face
We fight peers and pressures
Many things pass
But some things last forever
The last night loneliness
The unbelievable smiles that brighten days
The constant crying
Are some things that you will never forget
That great memory with a friend
The fussing about not being there
The all night calls
And the remarkable connection
You have a different moment than others
Marking your own grounds
Wanting to have help with the grounds
And a big hug for guidance
Just to be held tightly
Not knowing where or when
Striking that match
To rekindle the fire
Amounting to the storage of energy
Vanishing with the thin ice
Drying up an dying out
Making the environment a huge mistake
Seeing the candle go out
And hoping it will light up again
The pinch black room filled with emptiness
That you seem to always feel
Thinking you had a connection
But having nothing at all
Really hurts
You blink a number of times

But it's only true
You are alone
In the darkness
The feeling of emptiness
Is only real
And real it is
There is no escaping it now
You have to face reality
You only knew it would come some day
And when it did
You didn't expect it to be this hard on you
Now you sit and dream of a day
Where only you were happy
It seemed only true for a second
But when you woke
You trembled with hurt
Now you're standing alone once again
The hurt, pain and agony
When and where will it end?

FORGIVENESS

Have you ever known you were wrong and still asked for forgiveness?
Knowing that it was going to trigger an argument
Defeating the purpose of beginning the situation anyway
Knowing that it was going to come up that
You shouldn't have did it
What does asking for forgiveness really mean or what is forgiveness?
When you have a long day at work
And you automatically snap on a friend
And ask to be forgiven
Or when you and a friend have a long, hard argument that hurts
You ask for forgiveness
Times pass and you don't know how a friend feels
You pop off and say outrageous things that cause many problems
You want to be forgiven?
Asking for forgiveness isn't easy
When someone needs you bad
But you aren't there
Should you be given?
You cheat, lie and steal
Should you be forgiven?
You make a friend feel not wanted
Should that person forgive you?
If your friend commits suicide and it's your fault
Should I forgive you?
If you know a secret and you tell it
Should I think about forgiving?
If a friend wants honesty
And you lie
Should I forgive you?
They say you forgive and forget
But do you ever forget and should you forget?
Forgiving takes time
It's not like saying sorry
Which you always seem to be

Forgiveness comes from the heart
When a friend lets you down and isn't there
It takes a week or two
When a friend hurts you
It takes days
When a friend makes a mistake
It takes another mistake or two
When a friend isn't a friend
It takes many months
When a friend dies
It takes many moments alone
Forgiveness means hurt
Hurts mean to be forgiven
I knew I was wrong
But you don't always have to be right
Please forgive me

HEALING

The downpour of all the tears
The hurt
The emotion
The fear
The pain
The flashback of what happened
And what could happen
The experience
The things that are always unexpected
That hurt like hell
That hurt more than a knife through your heart
The feeling that you don't feel anymore
The things you see as you look in the mirror
The bags
The marks
The scars
The ugliness
Whatever that mattered before
Still matters now
But less
Seeing the hurt in the mirror
And it staring back
Makes it go deeper
Wounds are more surface
Underneath the wounds
The pain has now gone beyond skin deep
They can't see it but you can feel it
The hurt
The tears
The scars
The confusion
The first raw emotions that didn't involve death or evil thoughts
Just straight clarity that today was just one of those days
The emotions are expected

The hurt is to be expected
The feelings are raw
But today these feeling aren't of hurt
But these feelings are of healing
Of the healing that you never experienced before
But today
Today is a healing process

I DON'T CARE

The last time I checked you didn't care
Right now
You don't care
Take yourself and go somewhere else
The world will see you for who you are
And not for what things you put on
The more you talk
The deeper the hole
The more I think
The more I cry
I can't seem to escape the pain
Every time I turn around it's something new
Something…
Ugh…
Lack of sleep
Lack of concentration
I'm falling deeper
Wanting to dug my own hole
It's not that hard at this point
I think about what signs I ha
I never get the good sides of things
People leave me like I'm something
That has no value
But when they come back
There isn't going to a me to come back to
My feelings are raw
And I see no reason to care right now
I need to nurse myself back to health
Because they aren't going to do it
My face reveals many things
Many things that people can't see
But when I look in the mirror
I see the nights of worry
My voice tells it all

I'm hurt
But I always bounce back
It might take more time this time
But I don't care
Just as long as I heal
They will all miss me
I know it's for the best that I let go
It's the same old thing with every person I befriend
I love me and I love them
But now I have to live for me and move on
You didn't care
Now I don't care
I don't care

I THOUGHT

I thought about you today
When the river ran dry
And the tears fell down my face
About all the times you made me cry
And you left me feeling dry
I thought about you last night
When the sky was clear and the moon shined bright
About the times you made me laugh
And put a smile on my face
I thought about you this morning
When my alarm failed to ring
About all the times we stayed up all night talking about nothing
And failed to fall asleep
I thought about you a while ago
When I forgot to call to check up on you
About the times you never forget to call me
I thought of a place today
Where the raindrops were perfect
Reminding me of the way you tried to be
I dreamed of a place last night
Where my heart was broken and I hung myself
Reminding me of my many attempts
I went to a place this morning
Where I saw you making jokes with another friend
Reminding me of a friend I knew
I thought of many places together
When things only turned out right
About the times you never let me down
And things didn't turn out quite right
I thought of many things today that reminded me of you
But it seems to me that none of these things came true
I thought tonight that you were there till the end
Until I caught myself speaking to a friend
I see last week a friend in need

But never helped the shedding seize
I thought of a place
To keep at ease
To show a place to keep my plead
I think of you everyday
And I want to remain thinking of you
I thought of a poem today
That reminded me of you
Why is it that I thought to think of you?

Pretty in blue
Pretty in pink
The sadness on your face
As you look into someone's eyes
Your eyes
The eyes that are looking back at you
As you stare in the mirror
Looking at all your faults
Seeing the darkness in your eyes
The expression on your face
When you say "I'm pretty in pink"
But knowing that there is something missing
And that something is deeper than skin
Deeper than the expression on your face
The coldness you feel
When you stare into those eyes
And know that you're not the right color
Or the right size
But then second guessing yourself
Thinking about what's hiding underneath the makeup
And what's behind the smile
Knowing that you gave your all
And your all wasn't enough
Never is
The deep shadows that outline your eyes
And stain your skin
Seem permanent
Seem endless
Knowing maybe there was an escape
But sometimes things happen too late
And unexpected
No next times
Just the past

And what could have been
And now the end of it all
Just like the dark eyes that once said, “I’m pretty in pink”
Now say “I’m just me”

Just Me

LEAVING THIS

I tried telling myself things would be different
But things really aren't
That's the one thing I regret saying
It hurts knowing that but things happen
And it still happens to me
Maybe one day it will end
But then again
Taking that away
Is once in a lifetime chance
Seeing you and you seeing me
Seemed to right then
But now I have that feeling
That feeling that seeing you
Made my life ten times harder
Being held by you
Now seems like a mistake as well
Hearing your voice again
Will be the ultimate test
Will I need you?
Will I want you?
Or anything with you again?
Wanting to believe you want me is what I want
But actually hearing that is another story
That novel you see me as
Is only getting longer
The many pages that lie ahead are even more difficult
But knowing you are willing to take that risk
Wins major points with me
I can see all the things
You want from me
I'm willing to give them to you
But I'm just not ready for anything right now
My heart wants happiness
But then I see hurtfulness

Not from you but from me
I want to be promised a lot
But many things in me aren't guaranteed
You can take this and leave this
And I'm leaving this

LEFT

The last thing I remembered
Was seeing the sky turn gray
Laying there with no help
And knowing that I was left for dead
And then coming to
Was like someone was scaring me
The never seeing anything
Again was all I could think about
From the not doings
To the wish I dids
To the never will agains
It was finally to the point of no returns
When it came to the last
Final glance and gasp
The sky thundered
And the ground rumbled
My heart skipped one last beat
And faintly I whisper, "I love you all."
Saying that to anybody near
When I reached my destination
It was surrounded by people
That have hurt me
And I blinked twice to see if it was a dream
It felt more than real
One at a time would come
Up to me and explain
And every time
All I could do was cry
It brought back so many emotions and feelings
Taking two breaths
I awake back to real life
And someone's holding me
Tight and dear to their heart
I try looking up but my heart is compressed tightly to their body

Finally getting free
It's the one person I never thought would come to my rescue
Just in case I blinked twice
But the body stayed there
The only thing that was said
Kept playing over and over in my mind
"There, there, everything is going to be okay."
After they noticed that I was coming to
The tightness eased away
I fainted one last time
And this time I heard a voice saying
"I love you and that's all that matters, you're going to get through this."
By then I wanted to come out of my skin
I jumped out of the bed
And wanted to know where
All of this stuff came from
But at this time the body was gone
Left like all times before
Feeling weird and helpless
The hours passed
Along with a couple of days
That day faded away physically
But emotionally
All I could do was think and cry
Constantly
Once again I had been failed
And the failure
Was all I had felt lately
From the thinking I didn't care
To the hurting so much because I did care

LET THESE WORDS

Let these words flow
Like my fear flows
Freely and without hesitation
Let these words
Capture the heart of the unexpected
Let these words
By pass the fears
And cast a cloud over
My mind
Letting me know that fears
Are only temporary
Let these words
Take over and surprise the unexpected
Let my heart
Understand fears don't last forever
Let my mind
Capture the heart of 'The One'
The one that will fuss and still stay
The one that understands bad days
The one that stays even
When the doors are shut
Let these words
Tap dance on this paper
And leave an everlasting impression
Let these words
Flow as if someone else wrote them
As if someone else feels them
As if someone else can relate
Let these words
Be forever in your mind
Like they are forever in my heart
Let these words

Stand at attention
As if someone is saluting the paper
Let these words
Express my fears more than I can
Let these words
Show you how vulnerable one can be
Let these words
Show you the raw and rough
As I stand before you fed up and confused
Let these words
Show that I am me
And as me being me
I don't have any intentions of changing me
Take me or leave me
Because these words
Are the truth
And the truth is that I'm fed up
To the core with everybody
Let these words
Flow into your heart
And let you know that I'm serious
So serious
That it hurts
Let these words
Cast the blame on me
And only me
As the cloud clears up
And the sun shines bright
Let my words
Tell the story of not only me but others
Let these words
Show you how much caring for someone else hurts
Let these words
Show a sign of strength
That I never thought I had
Let these words

Embrace the embarrassed and ashamed soul
As the world judges you
Let these words…
Let these words…
Let these words…
Not only leave my mind
But fill your soul

NO MORE

I've tried so hard
To get that one thing
Maybe just someone to listen
I'm trying and trying
And still I try
But all I do is fall back
I've waited so long for someone to understand
And still I'm waiting
Why am I trying so hard to get that?
People see me and probably think
Whatever
I'm feeling like, what I want is to be….
And to want my life…
In that position where I don't want
Nobody to understand
And to careless if someone does care
I've fought and it's like I can't anymore
I take junk after junk
And I'm taking my last junk
They think but don't know
I know but don't care what they think
Everybody needs closure and reassurance
Soon and real soon
When I see my last….
And cry my last…
My doors will close then open
And open then shut
Questions will get their answers
And reactions will get a response
Ending the division
And beginning the…
I want to believe,
What I believe will happen

But how can I, if I have no signs
Crying isn't one of my answers, anymore
But crying will probably win
And beat all the odds and obstacles
That chapter has yet to start
But the end has come and gone
Breathing and blinking will put
Some of that pain behind
But my dreams and nightmares
Will surely help it return
Problems and issues
What are they?
The definitions to my life
Tears and fears of destruction
Constantly on point
Trying to keep calm and maintain
Staying out of anyone's way
And their concerns
Smiles, what do they do?
They hide all my misery
Help keep me as normal as possible
And show me that people do care
Constantly hiding my crazy ways
And releasing my false ways
Talking, talking, talking
Drama
Always something else with somebody
Conscience gets the best
And it always helps maintain the rest
Contemplating and wishing
It always end with a heart break
Things being…
And things that I see
Showing me that
That all I need is to be without that
Without all the misery
To forget and live one day at a time

And to take that deep and relieving breathe
No more thinking
No more…
Fighting but lost
Trying to close the doors of the understandings
And open the doors to the mystery mind

OBSERVE

Step back
Evaluate the situation
Don't ask
Just look and listen
Take note at your surroundings
Don't ask
Don't think
Just look
Enjoy the silence in your mind
Analyze how and what is around you
People don't always tell the whole truth
But actions speak
More than words ever will
Take note at that
One person
Look she speaks
But her speaking doesn't go with her actions
She is trying to convince herself of the words
Rather than you
She isn't confident
Her words are bland
Her eyes are low with no contact to you
She doesn't see you
She sees him
And her future going to waste
She is fighting to stay afloat
She hasn't told her friends
Due to the circumstances
She isn't 100 percent sure
Look at her attitude
Things have changed
But she hasn't fully told anybody
Don't judge her
Just love her

Just look
Notice the wording of her words
Notice the atmosphere she brings
Notice the confusion in her eyes
Wait until she tells you
Because secrets
Don't stay secrets for long
It's eating her alive
She can't sleep
She can't focus
Things have changed
Just look
Step back and observer
All things must come out
One way or another
Those 5 pounds didn't come from eating
They came from lack of sleep and rest
Stress will eat you alive
No judgment
Just listen and notice
Words can be deceiving
But actions never lie
Step back
Just observe

ONE

Him standing there
Her standing here
The sun sets
She runs
He follows
She turns
He turns
He stops
She runs
She's running for her life
He looks
Only the sun on the horizon
He sees
But can't feel
Can't touch
She runs
She sees the sun setting
But continues
She stops
She turns
Looks behind
He's not there
She looks
He's too far behind
He runs
To her touch
But the touch is farther than the sun
She wants to run into his arms
But his arms
Stopped too
She runs back to him
He looks
Sees
He grabs

Her waist
They join
Become one
With one
They become
He ran
She ran
He turns
She turns
And into each other's arms
They stand
As one
One

Looking for the right words to describe you
It's hard
But just thinking about what we have makes a smile form
Seeing you smile
Brings even more happiness
From talking about nothing
To talking about everything
The next day draws interest
Sometimes you can be a pain
But other days you're sweet
Sometimes I wish I never met you
But then again that's not what I really mean
Seeing stars makes me think
Of how bright you make my day
Seeing the clear blue sky
Makes me think about how clear and blank my minds gets
When I hear your voice
To seeing the dark gloomy night
Makes me think about how I feel
When you act so unintelligent
Stars, skies, nights and smiles
All remind me of at least one part of you
What reminds you of me?
Reminders

SEE THROUGH

The look in their eyes that they see what you feel
Never realizing that it was that obvious
I see somebody that has nothing but her
But is always making sacrifices
People say I should smile more
But when I want to
I start thinking
And when I start thinking I start crying
And when I cry I start worrying
You never realize what and why things happen until
Until after the lesson is over
Whose fault was it?
I should live but why
Nobody likes me
It's only me
I'm not putting myself out there again
My wall is back up
I don't care what people think
But in honesty I do care what people think
It's always going to be something in their mind
The look in their eyes that they see what you feel
Never realizing that your feelings where that transparent

SILENCE

Silence could mean many things
The confused look
Displayed on her eyebrows
The tone of her voice
The pitch of her laugh
They both are fake
Altered
Something isn't right
The silence you display
Silence
Take notice
All things are not what they seem
Silence can be shown
Shown in the expression of her eyes
No tone
No expression
No emotion
That evil grin
Silence can fall on her heart
She is silent to fill that void of love
To fill that emptiness feeling
Confused
Silence
The way the conversation is one sided
The way you look at her as she tries to convince herself of the lie
Silence
Don't let any form of silence rest in your area
Silence

STRESS

It rises
Settles in your shoulders
Starts running up and down your body
It starts as casual pain
You wave it off
It gets worse
You wave it off
It starts to spread
You take 2 Advil
It relieves it for 2 days
It returns
You take 2 more Advil
And disregard the pain
3 days later
Still having pain
You walk and stand dead center in front of the mirror
You stand still
No movement at all
You notice the stress
The strain in your eyes
You're tired
The pain that settled in your shoulders
Its stress
The stress
Of holding on to something that doesn't want to be held any longer
Those 2 Advil
Did nothing
Because you tried to avoid the real issue
The real reason
The tension
That is resting on your soul
On your chest
In your heart

Let it go
Those bags and dark lines under your eyes
Yes those
They have formed
From the unhappiness
The pain that is settling
In your shoulders
It's not visible
But it's physical
Release it
Stop trying to mask the pain
Let it go

TAKE THIS

Take the time
And ask my name
It's what you want it to be
Sweet, sweet
The way things happen
And they happen for a reason
Look inside your heart
And see what you find
Maybe a feeling to be loved
Or cared for
Or wanted, held
Take that mind and that soul
And empty it onto someone else
Go love someone else
Just feel half of what the movie stars feel
Hurt for a minute at a time
Or an hour
It takes time
Take time to learn
My name
And call it right
The first time
It hurts to be loved
Love hurts
Just a little at a time
But the love will ease
Take the time
To love me
You might miss your chance
That would hurt
Take the time to miss me
To show me you care
Just a little

Maybe even a lot
Enough to get by
To look me in my eyes
And capture me
Take me away
Maybe even take my breathe away
Take the time to show you care
In your heart,
Your eyes,
Your mind,
Your soul,
Your body
I want it all to be mine for a second
To be intertwined with me for a moment
Where I feel nothing but us
Take the time to
Cherish in me
What I cherish in you
The you being you
All of you
The love, kindness, heart, soul
What I need
Take the time to see
In me
What I can't seem to find
That…
Completeness
That completeness
Where I can finish something right
And start something right
Take the time to just
Hold me tight
This time before you go!...
Take the time to…
See what I see in you!

I walk that extra mile for you
I'll talk that extra word for two
I'll clean my room just for you
Last night I sang that extra tone
Waiting for you to ring the phone
I try not to worry
But all I can do is hurry
Hurry I ran that mile
Just to see that glittering smile
I fought to make it there in time
But instead I committed a crime
You told me love wasn't in your vocabulary
But instead I fell for you
You touched me so I should not worry
You said sorry
But were you sorry?
I'll make that extra mile
Only for you
But you fake that smile
All I wanted was to feel
But instead I felt the shame
Walking an extra mile for you
Only to get broken in two
Committing crimes
I love you deeply
Dreaming of only you
And writing to only you
Feeling that smile
I keep running that mile
Losing that pound or two
Just to please you
That extra mile I walked
But I would never crawl
I would cry during that mile

But never would I give up
To the end I go
But little do you know that I do hate you now
That mile
Shined through me
Grew brighter
And grew lighter
My heart fell through
And my mind hurt too
That extra mile
Added a fake smile
I cried for days
Until I could find them better days
I wanted to walk that extra mile
But I couldn't find the pace again
I failed to love another
But I didn't fail to drop another tear
I heard
You ran a mile for me
But why not with a crying plea?

That Extra Mile

The sun rises
Then falls
The music sets the mood
Bringing all the tension to the surface
But every mood and song
Has its past time
The things that have happened
Or are yet to happen
Some faults
Some miracles
Some in between
The moon trades with the sun
You trade with her
The shades change
The temperatures
Just like when trading with her
Standing there looking over your shoulder
Always
Feeling less
Maybe different
All the looks
All the feelings
When the sun rises on the opposite side
So do you
The mood isn't right
Nothing is
The thoughts, the wishes, the hopes
Knowing the outcome of it all
Of all the things that live inside
And those things are taking over
Your body
Your life
Your soul
Your heart

The emptiness
Of not feeling wanted
And not knowing something has to end
And soon
Maybe sooner than later
Opening new doors
And closing curtains
When the moon still shines brightly
The upside
Is a downside
The downside
Is a upside

THE FIGHT

I put in too much
I'm weak and helpless
My life is full of unsolved mysteries
I try to solve all possible
But my answer is never fully stated
I get mixed feelings
Misused and misled
My time valuable
Things fall in and out of place
My mind is off track
I look dead and feel the same
Crying and talking
But nothing is clear
Not even the date
I wake and reality awaits
Problems have attracted to me
Like friction
I fall and give up
It's over
The fight has ended and I've lost
The things that mattered most
Have died out
Along with my hope
I put in but it didn't put out
It's finished, done, over
The battle is resolved
And I'm alone, estranged, isolated
Caring less, now
My tears dry up
And my eyes turn red
I glance for a second
And find myself in a whirl of tears
Trying to hide, but it's too late

Turning heads, people staring
Caring no more
Just minding my business
Getting pulled aside by a force
Something happens
And it eases my mind
But I never forget
My cries return
But finally subside
My reasons are explained
In my emotions
I love, care and dislike
But learn to understand
And say whatever
It's taking away some hurt
But also causing hurt
Experiencing loneliness
But it's making progress
A little more everyday
I've learned and lost
But I'm letting the fight win

The one day things seem right
Things are right
The weather is right
And all my moods are fight
I smiled today
Having one that really was a smile
Not fake
But it seemed too real
I'm staying strong
And I'm trying not to shed a tear
I know I have a fear
That only my inner soul can overcome
I'm fighting that bad seed off
Because I want that day to be just right
I just told
I'm always depressed
This is for you
My day is great
And I love smiling
Why can't I have many more days to myself?
I'm doing okay
To others
I may look stressed
A migraine today
Is kicking like crazy
But I'm trying to live with it today
Just to be a little normal
And worry about nothing today
To you I dedicate this to
To me I dedicate a better day
Thanks to you I'm doing better
With migraine and all
I never thought a person
Could mean so much to me

When it comes to a better way
I'm glad you love and care that much
For a person like me
The one thing today was all but right
I never thought today could be so right

SKY

The sky falls
And along came the sun
I fall
And along came my fun
The many different things that happen are all but nice
You wish upon a star
And the star has no happiness
I wanted the star for myself
And the star was already dedicated
Last week the star fell
And my wish came true
The sun rose and so did the sky
When it fell I was there
When it rose I was more than there
And when I leave, I'll leave you a magical cloud
The clouds cover my smiles
And the sky shows my hurt
Many times I wish there was
No more hurt
But when the clouds cover
I all but hurt
The days fall harder
And the smiles shine brighter
You owe me your life
But I'll take an apology
When you never remembered
I never forgot
And then we both had our excuses
Why replace the don't haves
With I can't have
And have the many stars fall with hurt
I stopped short

And had no sort of assurance
When the sky falls
I fall
And along came the sun
With all the covering clouds

THE WAY IT HAPPENED

As I hear you rise
My heart gently cries
All the things I remember you saying
The one thing I remember most is,
"I love you, I love you, I really do"
The many ways you make me smile
I take a bow
You always know how to take the breath out of me
I fainted the last time I seen you
You gently eased your hands around my waist
I feel you rubbing my back
As I drifted off and away
To a place so high that as I reached
It my head started doing a dance
My heart skips a beat
And my eyes fill with water
As gently as I went away
Is the same way I came back
"Take me; take me now to a place where I'm loved with all my ailments"
Where seeing myself in a mirror isn't
Like looking inside a death trap
"I love you now, I'll love you forever"
Speaking those words are like
Hypnotizing me in my little world
I see your face
And in that face I see a cheater
You cheated on me
And I thought you said, "I love you, I love you, I really do"
My heart died
And it went away
And when it went away
All I seen was you
Taking what I thought was real away
The tears didn't fall down my face

But they filled your face
I felt no pity for you
But for me
Because the facts of seeing you,
Knowing you hurt
But my heart and soul died
"I love you now and I'll love you forever" will be the words that will stick
With me
And I'll love you too
But I'm not in love with you
You're not for me and I'm not for you
"Take me; take me now to a place where I'm loved"
The tears fell
But they fell in buckets

THERE MAY BE A TWICE

If things would once go away I would find a smile and cry in the same state
I miss all the times I used to have
Where I could smile or be happy without being asked why
I miss all the things I used to have during the day
I miss having a smile at least once a day
I miss being myself and understanding myself
I just miss all the things before now
When I think about what things I have now
I cry and continue to cry until I get tired
But eventually it comes back
And I continue to cry
When things come down to getting rough
I start missing the times when my life was so easy
The no crying nights and the constant smiles that weren't fake
If things were once like I prayed
Then there would be no reason to pray anymore
I promised if I cried and laughed in the same state
It would be my last time
But that promise was broken
Crying then laughing at the same state of mind
Isn't something I should be proud of
And it isn't something I'm proud of
Going through the motions
Only makes my days harder
If things would once go my way
Then there may be a twice
Then I could stop missing and misunderstanding myself

Stepping in them
Empowers a new personality
Its like magic
Head heal high
Eye contact
Feet no longer dragging the floor
Confidence
Not cocky
Yet confident with a slight new step
The feel
The glow
The ability
The spirit
Its like POW Pow
The enery is different
The surroundings are different
Walking is on a whole
New level
New dress
New hairstyle
Same person
But those HEELS they said
"POW! POW!! POW!!!"
Those heels

TIRED

I am tired
Not of life
Just exhausted
Mentally and physical
The words
"I am tired"
Could generate many things
But my "I am tired"
Means just that
Means that I am over exerted
Over extended
Overwhelmed
I am here
Here on this earth
I am fighting
Fighting for a better day
A better later
I'm not here
To complain
But I am here to speak my truth
I am tired
Because I need to take a moment
To enjoy life
And not work so hard to provide a life
I am tired
Are you tired?

TO WAIT

Pure happiness
Pure tears of joy
Pure laughter
No confusion
No doubts
Consistence
The ability to argue
Get mad
And still talk later that day
Pure joy
Pure acknowledgment of your presence
Pure unconditional love
The ability to know what you feel without hearing the words
The ability to know that you want me
That you only see me
That you see me with my flaws and all
The ability to understand my hurt and not question it
The pure excitement
From hearing your name
The pure acknowledgment from seeing your face
The pure understanding that all of the others were just others
And that I waited this long for the golden prize
The ability to look in your eyes and see my future
To see my future not only with you
But my future brighter
The ability to smile with knowing that as I write these words
That these words are for you
The ability to know that all the others missed out
That all the others were only stepping stones
In order for us to be together
No comparisons
No insecurities
No disrespect
No hurtfulness

Communication
Commitment
Dedication
Love
Desire
Pure happiness
Pure commitment
Pure love
Pure laughter
Are the things that I see I you
The pleasure of know I didn't settled
And that I waited for all the right reasons

Every unfinished line
Every unfinished thought
They are filled with constant mind burners
Not being able to understand
The understandable
The vulnerability of the mind
Getting lost in every breath
Every second
The chance you don't get think about the present
To wish on the future
And pray on the past
Knowing that sometimes the past isn't always that
Dreaming about the knowabouts
And the whatabouts
Knowing that the mended heart is now a broken heart
The unfinished ties
The unfinished business
Burns a hole on your insides
The constant nagging that doesn't go away
Until you go away
Knowing that it's one thing or another
Then the constant reminder that everybody has problems
They just don't dwell on them
Don't dwell on them
Unfinished lines
Unfinished thoughts
If they love you
They will love all of you
Unfinished or not

STOP

You feel that
That heartbeat is your purpose
Yesterday is gone
Today is here
Enjoy every moment
The simple things
Like being able to smell the flowers
Being able to see
Being able to feel
Being able to touch
Being able to breathe
Stop
You feel that
That is your reason for being

WHAT GOOD IS LOVE....

What good is love, when you can't feel the presence of the other person?
What good is love, when the more you it the more emotionally hurt you get?
What good is love, when it fails you instead of making things better?
Love hurts like hell
But it always finds a way to fail somebody
What good is love....
When the one you love loves somebody else?
What good is love, when you can't find true love?
What good is love when the one you love doesn't trust you?
What good is love when it just doesn't seem real anymore?
What good is love when you have gave up on love?
What good is love, when everything else fails you?
What good is love to you?

Standing in front of me stands
What?
What stands in front of you?
I stand stronger today than yesterday
Fighting to enjoy life more than yesterday
In my mind stands
Stands a strong, loving, independent, caring, young woman
I have fought for everything I have
I stand in front of the mirror
Knowing that hurt in my eyes
Will only last a short period of time
But that light that reflects and shines through
Will prevail
I never question why one thing happens to me now
I never question when things don't happen
I live for the moment
Because today is the present
Yesterday is history
And tomorrow isn't guaranteed
I stand
Knowing I have become who I want to be
Working on myself daily
But I am ready for the next challenge, commitment
So what stands in front of you?

WHAT WILL THE NEXT HOUR BRING?

Today I lost one
But I know what tomorrow brings
It brings no hope, no time, nothing
The I almost got lost
And the I'm so sorry
It doesn't make up for the things I lost
The apology made me cry
And you look in my eyes
And I just want to die
The flashing back
Only made the tears deepen
But knowing I'm secure
Helps me remain focused
Seeing you cry
Makes me feel like the world's ending
The crying you feel
Is the same dying I feel
The endless hugs
And the remarkable talks
Put a smile on my heart
But me losing one today
Is like never seeing the sun shine again
But when the clouds are bright
And the stars shine all night
My life is still lost
But today I lost my soul
And someone else's heart
All I want to know is
What will the next hour bring?

When you realize that things are bad
Is when reality strikes you dead in the heart?
Staring in your face for days at a time
Waiting for you to make your next decision
If you want to escape or stay?
Making things lost because things could get better or just because
It's all on you
The things that you once wanted aren't there
And never were
It's taking the easy way out
But we all make choices
Choices we have to stick and live with
Thinking what's the use?
But knowing it's not worth it in the end
It's hurting you and knowing that
Is the obvious thing
Escape and live with that
Because that's more important than staying
But what does instinct know?
Nothing
Stay?
And live with what you know as
The hurts, cries and lies
It could get better sooner or later, Right?
Knowing but not believing
That's the problem
When does this stop?
The things that don't get understood
The things that are misread
The thing aren't seen
They are all things that you know
But aren't believing
They are all things reality is trying to tell you
What's your next move?

WHY CAN'T I LET GO

Why can't I let go?
Taking medicine is an everyday routine for some
Others for their own use
I used to think my life couldn't go on
But it has yet to end
My mind has stopped
But my heart keeps pumping
Love, is what it is
And sometimes it is what is isn't
Hearts get broken
And are yet to be mended
I want to stop fighting
But I know I can't let go
I can't let go
Because times do show
That you have been good to me
But you break my poor heart
And expect me to not leave
You touch me with your words
And I almost break
I touch you with my pain
And you could care less
You hold me without holding me
Many days I see your face
And wish that there were better days
Days without you
Are hours without sleep
I can't let go
Because I've cried too much
And fought too much for you
My heart wants that one last hug before I go
Are you going to let go?
I wonder just why I can't let go
Is it that I don't want anybody else to have you?

Or is it that I still have deep feelings for you?
You stuck by my side
During my emotional times and a few great times
I'm holding you close
Without holding you
You're blowing me off
And I still can't let go
My mind wants to end it all
But my heart is still holding on
You have a piece of it
And I can't get hold of it
My heart is crying out
Why can't I just let go?
You hurt me
And still I stay
I'm holding on to your thoughts and words
But now I'm letting go
Why can't I let go?
Because you won't let me go
I held on and now it has failed
My tears fell for you last night
That is and was your last night
I'm holding on no more
And it's time to let go
But why can't I let go?

Never ask why someone is put into your life to take care of you
Always ask why not?
Why not take care of you?
This pain is unbearable
But I'm pushing forward
This will not define my life
I can't live in fear of this disease
It's not going to take over my life
I am stronger than this
You will not take over my life
I am stronger than you
I am stronger than you
You will not take over my life

I AM WORTHY

I stopped asking myself why
And started asking why not me
I am worthy
I am passionate about life
I show understanding
I forgive when needed
I cry
I laugh
I smile
I love
I am worthy
So why not me
I stand faced by negativity and false pretenses
But I know deep down inside
The false pretenses are only insecurities
That need to be solved, internally
I understand that mistakes are made
But I also understand that after the second mistake
It's no longer a mistake
That it is indeed intentional
I need understanding
But I also need love
And with both life is so much smoother
I love with my all
Until the love in people fails me
Why not me I say
I trust
Until I'm crosses incorrectly
I listen
Until my ears bleed
I see
Until my eyes cross

I breathe
Until I breaths within get shallow
I wonder without reason
So why not me
I am worthy

Would you ever lie to a friend?
Would you ever lie to a friend to spare their feelings?
The feeling of having someone lie to you isn't pleasant
If you lie about how that dress looks
Then would you lie about being their friend?
Is a question, a question that gets asked randomly
Or is an everyday experience that needs to be answered?
I wonder everyday
Would one of my friends lie to me?
Maybe?
I know many have
But that's why they aren't my friends anymore
It shows that not everybody is your friend
And not everybody will have your best interest at heart
You may say "Nobody will do me like that"
But next week
You'll have a complete change of heart
Maybe your friend made
A smart comment
And they claim they didn't say it
But you knew they were lying
Because you were standing about three feet away
Minding your own business
Or the person said they were going to call
But never did
And when you asked where they were
They say something like, "I had to work late"
But you know they are lying
Because you both work at the same place and she left way before you did
Why lie to a good friend or a friend about anything?
Lying will only led to a broken heart
That later you will have to mend
Just be honest
You have to spend your time mending a heart

Then when would you actually have time to have a real talk
You wonder if your friend lies
Then are they a friend
Everyday it's a question of life or death
I would rather speak the truth
And lose a friend
Than lie and hurt a friend
But then you think "would they tell the truth"
You never know
But it hurts to be wrong
When you know that they should be right
Meaning harm is never hard to see
But meaning honesty can always be harmful to feel
Would you ever lie to a friend to spare their feelings?
Only you know what's in your heart
Keep what you feel all real
And you and only you
Can tell what you really feel
Then a friend can help mend whatever
A friend can mean the world to you
And lying can hurt the friend the most
Why lie to a friend about anything?

You are you
And I am me
We're different
But yet we have a lot in common
One day I have an attitude
The next you have one
Helping one another is another common interest
The many things we have shared
But the many things we have feared
Wishing upon a star
But then not knowing why
Our friendship ended
But our bond still stands strong
I see your face in my dreams
But I don't feel your presence
The feeling is so sick
My heart is empty
But deep in my soul
I know you're there
It's like Romeo and how Juliet felt
Your heart is still here literally
But your body is in many distance dreams
The bond we share is thicker than peanut butter
If peanut butter can stay together
So can we
I am me
And you are you

YOU CAN'T KEEP TRYING TO TELL YOURSELF YOU LOVE THIS PERSON...

Open your eyes
Turn around
And look in front of you
What always looks good on the outside
Ain't always good on the inside
Search for that soul
That everyone deserves
You keep trying to tell yourself that you love this person
But what is love?
Love isn't always hurt
Love is caring
Love is calling
Loving knows that what that person feels is real
Love isn't cheating
Then lying about it
Love isn't being repaired with someone else
But it's working through the hardships
And fighting for what you have
Putting your right foot first
And loving through
Thick and thin
Everyone makes mistakes
But you can't keep trying to tell yourself that you love someone
You feel love
Love is a feeling
When that person isn't there
Your heart throbs
For wanting them
Wanting to be close

Wanting to know they care
Wanting to hold them in your arms
But love is sometimes
Misunderstood
Misunderstood as hate
There's a thin line between love and hate
Being done wrong every chance they get
Isn't love
Being fussed at
Slammed...
You can't keep trying to tell yourself that you love someone
Let them tell you
Show you that night out on the town
And love all your faults
Because you aren't perfect
But they aren't either
Let them love you
A little at a time
To show that
That there is learning in process
Let their heart throb for
A little
To show that
They are living
You can't keep trying to tell yourself you love someone
You either do
Or you don't
When you miss them as soon as you leave their sight
Or hang up the phone
Just the simplest things still make you happy
And that genuine smile
Makes you glow on the inside and out
Love is making them smile
When their day
Just isn't going right
Giving them just what they need
Some ears to listen

And not feedback
Just being there
And love being there
You can't keep trying to tell yourself you love this person
Because you will know!

Once you empty your heart of all the unnecessary heartache
You will fill it with so much happiness
You can't make someone else's problem yours
You can't carry the load of someone else
When that someone else is only out for self
You can't make someone happy
When you are unhappy
You can't care
When they could careless
You can't make it work
You can't make them stay
You can't make them talk
You can't make them cry
You can't make them understand
You can't make them your priority
You can't understand the struggle
Until you feel the pain
You can't make this about you
When it's about me
You can't make this yours
When its mine
You can't
You can't
You just can't.....

YOU TOLD ME

You told me things would get better
Things got worse
You told me I had nothing to worry about
I worried
You told me you will never leave me
You left
You told me you would always be there
You never were
You told me I didn't need to cry
I cried
You told me I had a friend
I had none
You told me we would make it through
We barely made it
I told you I would never leave you
I stayed clear
I told you, you had a friend
You had tons
I told you I would need you
I needed you
I told you I would always be there
I never left
I told you, you were special
You are
I told you I was tired of trying
I gave up
I told you I needed time
You told me you needed space
I told you
Mine came true
You told me
It just wasn't meant for me

YOUR needs to be US
Your vision
Your dream
Your reality
Your feelings
Your personality
Your mind
Your eyes
Your legs
Your body
Your success
Your mindset
Your everything
Everything is your
When everything should be
Our instead of your
Your can't build us a future
Your needs to be us
Your can't take up the space of our time
Your can't make us a stable us
Your will become a problem
Your will take over us
Your will be lonely
You need to make that your us
And let us fight for us
Your vision
Our vision
Your personality
Our personalities
Our team
All of your needs to be us or our

ABOUT THE AUTHOR

It all started with me writing to express my emotions—until I realized that my words actually spoke the silent inner voice of someone else. I started getting excited about writing, and when new ideas would pop up in my mind, I realized this was meant for me: that this was my gift.

I have been writing poetry since I was in middle school, and that's when I realized I wanted to write a book and be published. I have three short stories that I wrote in high school, which I have hidden away.

I am a twenty-seven-year-old from a small town in North Carolina that has a vision to one day have a book in the bookstore.

CPSIA information can be obtained
at www.ICGtesting.com
Printed in the USA
FFOW02n2035160215
11155FF

9 781496 94570